W9-DDG-864

A DICTIONARY OF
DINOSAURS

by
Rupert Matthews

Illustrated by
Chris Forsey

Derrydale Books

New York

Acanthopholis

— Acanthopholis —
(Ah-can-thoff-oll-iss)

Acanthopholis was a plant-eating dinosaur. "Dinosaur" is the name given to a group of reptiles that lived from 225 to 65 million years ago but completely died out. There are no dinosaurs alive today. Acanthopholis was longer than a small truck and had bony plates along its back. It lived in Britain about 120 million years ago.

— Albertosaurus —
(Al-ber-tow-saw-rus)

Albertosaurus was a large, powerful meat-eating dinosaur that lived about 70 million years ago. It was about 30 feet long and stood twice as tall as a man. It most probably attacked and killed other dinosaurs for food, using its long, sharp teeth and the fierce talons on its hind legs as weapons. The scientific name for a meat-eater is a "carnivore." It was lightly built and was probably able to run quickly.

Albertosaurus means "reptile from Alberta" and it was called this because its preserved bones – called fossils – were found in Alberta, Canada. Fossils are the bones, teeth and other remains of extinct animals, which have been trapped in rock and, over millions of years, have turned to stone. Fish and plant fossils also exist.

Albertosaurus

Anatosaurus

Allosaurus

Allosaurus
(Al-owe-saw-rus)

Allosaurus lived for a long time during what fossil experts call the late Jurassic period. This was from 195 to 135 million years ago. This enormous creature – it was about 39 feet long – was a good hunter and could attack other large dinosaurs. It walked on its hind legs and was rather agile for its size. Its long, sharp teeth were serrated like steak knives and its short front legs had sharp claws that were useful for attacking prey.

Anatosaurus
(An-at-owe-saw-rus)

Anatosaurus was a duck-billed dinosaur. It had a horny beak at the front of its head. It was about 40 feet long and lived in North America 70 million years ago.

Anchisaurus
(An-kee-saw-rus)

Anchisaurus lived about 200 million years ago, earlier than most other dinosaurs. Its fossils have been found in North America and Africa. This small dinosaur, about 6 feet long, was very slim and agile, allowing it to escape from predators. Anchisaurus had short blunt teeth, which indicates that it ate plants. The scientific name for a plant-eater is a "herbivore." Its strong legs and sharp claws made it possible for this dinosaur to catch small animals.

Anchisaurus

Ankylosaurus

Ankylosaurus

(An-kee-low-saw-rus)

This plant-eating dinosaur was found in North America and lived about 70 million years ago. Ankylosaurus was as large as a tank and was covered in thick, bony armor, which protected it from being attacked by meat-eating dinosaurs. Even its eyelids were plated with bone! Ankylosaurus had a huge club-shaped bone at the end of its tail. Large, powerful muscles were attached to the tail to swing the tail-club around. If an Ankylosaurus were attacked, it could defend itself with its tail-club.

Archaeopteryx

(Ar-kee-op-ter-icks)

Archaeopteryx was not truly a dinosaur but is the earliest known bird. It lived about 150 million years ago in central Europe. Archaeopteryx had feathers and wings like a bird but teeth and a bony tail like a reptile. Its ancestors were reptiles and over many thousands of years developed into birds. Archaeopteryx was as big as a crow, and fed on small animals such as insects and lizards. This early bird's wings were quite weak, and it probably was not a good flyer. Some scientists think that Archaeopteryx was related to small dinosaurs, such as Compsognathus. If they are right, then all birds are related to the ancient dinosaurs.

Apatosaurus

(Ah-pat-owe-saw-rus)

Apatosaurus was a huge, plant-eating dinosaur. It was 69 feet long and weighed up to 30 tons. It lived about 140 million years ago in North America. Apatosaurus used its long neck to reach the treetops where it gathered leaves to eat. This dinosaur's tail was very long too, and ended in a thin whiplash. Scientists used to call it Brontosaurus until they realized that the Brontosaurus fossils were the same as those of the dinosaur called Apatosaurus. Since a dinosaur cannot be called by two different names, Apatosaurus was chosen.

Brachiosaurus
(Brack-ee-owe-saw-rus)

Brachiosaurus was so tall that it could have looked over the tops of most modern houses. It lived about 135 million years ago in eastern Africa. Brachiosaurus was a plant-eating dinosaur. By virtue of its long neck, Brachiosaurus could reach higher than most other animals. Its teeth were short and shaped like pegs, which is how we know that it ate leaves. Unlike most dinosaurs, Brachiosaurus had front legs that were longer than its hind legs. This gave Brachiosaurus its name, which means "arm reptile."

Brontosaurus
(Bron-tow-saw-rus)

Brontosaurus fossils were discovered in North America in 1879. Because of the way that its skeleton was reconstructed, it took until 1975 for the scientists to realize that Brontosaurus was the same as Apatosaurus (see opposite).

Apatosaurus

Archaeopteryx

Brachiosaurus

Cc

Camarasaurus

Camptosaurus

Camptosaurus
(Camp-tow-saw-rus)

This dinosaur could grow up to 23 feet long and was found in Europe and North America where it lived 145 million years ago. Camptosaurus walked on its hind legs most of the time, but sometimes traveled on all fours when feeding. It was one of the first plant-eating dinosaurs to have cheeks. This important development meant that it could chew its food properly before swallowing. Most successful plant-eating dinosaurs had cheeks.

Camarasaurus
(Cam-ar-ah-saw-rus)

Camarasaurus was a large plant-eating dinosaur, about 59 feet long. It ate leaves from the lower branches of trees. It had massive pillar-shaped legs that were strong enough to carry the enormous weight of the dinosaur. Camarasaurus lived about 140 million years ago in North America.

Ceratosaurus

Cetiosaurus

Cetiosaurus

(Set-ee-owe-saw-rus)

Cetiosaurus was similar in many ways to Apatosaurus. It was a large, plant-eating dinosaur and lived in Europe and Africa about 150 million years ago.

Chasmosaurus

(Chass-mow-saw-rus)

Chasmosaurus was one of the first horned dinosaurs. It lived about 80 million years ago in North America. Chasmosaurus's horns were rather small, but the frill around its neck was very big. Scientists think that horned dinosaurs such as this one only used their horns for defense, not for attacking other animals.

Chasmosaurus

Ceratosaurus

(Sir-at-owe-saw-rus)

Ceratosaurus was a meat-eating dinosaur that lived in the same place as Camptosaurus. Ceratosaurus may have hunted Camptosaurus, attacking with its sharp teeth and powerful arms. It was about 20 feet long and could run quickly. It probably hunted in packs. Ceratosaurus was the only meat-eating dinosaur to have a horn on its nose. Experts do not know exactly what this was for but suspect it might have been used as a weapon or was simply just for show.

Chialingosaurus

— Chialingosaurus —
(Chiy-al-in-go-saw-rus)

This dinosaur lived 150 million years ago in China. It was as long as a car, and was very slender. The plates on its back may have acted as protective armor.

— Coelophysis —
(See-low-fizz-is)

A small, fast hunter, Coelophysis lived in North America 210 million years ago and preyed upon lizards and smaller animals. It scampered about on its long hind legs and used its front legs to catch prey. Its mouth was full of small, needle-sharp teeth ideal for biting its food.

Coelophysis

Coelurus

— Coelurus —
(See-loo-rus)

This small dinosaur was around 6 feet tall. It had long legs which helped it run very quickly and catch small lizard-like animals for food. Coelurus lived about 140 million years ago in North America.

Compsognathus

Compsognathus
(Comp-sog-nay-thus)

Compsognathus is the smallest adult dinosaur ever found. It lived in Europe about 140 million years ago and was only about the size of a chicken. This tiny creature was very agile and ran quickly on its hind legs. The front legs were short with three small claws on each hand. Compsognathus may have hunted small animals in dense undergrowth, using its front legs to hold its prey. Scientists believe it might also have been a scavenger. When a large meat-eating dinosaur made a kill, Compsognathus would have snatched a mouthful of meat and then run quickly away.

Corythosaurus

Corythosaurus
(Corry-thow-saw-rus)

Up to 33 feet long – as long as three cars parked end-to-end, this dinosaur ate very tough plant food such as pine needles and twigs. We know that Corythosaurus ate food like this because a fossil of its stomach has been found containing pine needles and twigs. It needed a remarkable mouth to eat this food. It had a hard beak at the front, which was useful for biting twigs from trees. The teeth behind the beak were used to chew on tough food. Corythosaurus had hundreds of teeth, arranged in long rows on both sides of its mouth. Each tooth was ridged and able to crush the hardest foods. This made Corythosaurus a very successful dinosaur. It survived in North America from about 90 million years ago until 70 million years ago.

Dd

Daspletosaurus
(Daz-plet-owe-saw-rus)

The name Daspletosaurus means "frightful reptile," which is a very good description of this ancient reptile. A relative of Tyrannosaurus, it preyed upon other dinosaurs. Daspletosaurus grew up to 30 feet long and lived 70 million years ago in North America.

Daspletosaurus

Deinonychus

Deinonychus
(Day-non-ee-kus)

Deinonychus was a fast-running hunter that lived about 120 million years ago in North America. It was around 10 feet long and was probably the most dangerous meat-eating dinosaur of its time. When it attacked other dinosaurs, Deinonychus used the two large, sharp, curved claws on its hind feet. Scientists think the Deinonychus may have balanced on one hind foot, while it slashed its prey to death with the claw on the other. Then it used its big teeth to tear off lumps of meat.

Dicraeosaurus
(Dye-cray-owe-saw-rus)

Dicraeosaurus was what scientists call a sauropod dinosaur – one that ate plants, had a small head and long neck and tail, and had five-toed limbs. It lived in Africa during the Jurassic period, 195 to 135 million years ago. Dicraeosaurus grew to 42 feet long.

Dicraeosaurus

Dilophosaurus
(Dill-off-owe-saw-rus)

Dilophosaurus was a large meat-eater that lived 180 million years ago. It was a very unusual dinosaur as it had two thin crests of bone on top of its skull. These crests were very fragile, and probably would soon have broken if used for weapons. Some scientists think that the crests may have been used to signal to other Dilophosauruses in the same manner that peacocks signal to each other with their tails.

Dilophosaurus

Dimorphodon
(Dye-morf-owe-don)

Dimorphodon was a very early flying reptile. These flying animals are not really dinosaurs, but are called "pterosaurs." Dimorphodon lived about 180 million years ago in Britain. With its long legs, and a tail that was used for balance, this flyer might also have been a good runner.

Dimorphodon

Diplodocus
(Dip-lod-owe-cus)

With a length of 88 feet, Diplodocus was one of the longest dinosaurs known. This is about as long as eight cars parked end-to-end! However, it was not one of the heaviest dinosaurs but was rather slim. Most of its length was made up by its thin neck and tail. Diplodocus ate plants, and used its long neck to reach leaves in the tops of tall trees, just as a giraffe does today. It lived in North America about 140 million years ago.

Diplodocus

—— Dromaeosaurus ——
(Drom-ee-owe-saw-rus)

This dinosaur was about 6 feet tall – the same height as a man. It was a ferocious, fast-running hunter and probably attacked dinosaurs about the same size as itself, such as Dromiceiomimus. It may also have eaten small creatures such as lizards and mammals. The sharp claws on its hind legs were used to slash at large prey. Dromaeosaurus ran on its hind legs, holding its tail stiff, which helped to balance the weight of its body.

—— Dromiceiomimus ——
(Drom-iss-ee-owe-my-mus)

Dromiceiomimus was one of the fast-running creatures called "ostrich dinosaurs." As you can see from the picture, it has the shape of an ostrich with a tail. Dromiceiomimus measured 10 to 13 feet from head to tail tip, and lived about 70 million years ago in Canada. It was able to run as fast as a modern horse and may have been the swiftest of all dinosaurs. Well-built for speed, the hind legs were long, slender, and powered by immensely strong muscles. The whole body was very light. Dromiceiomimus could escape its enemies by running away at high speed.

Dromaeosaurus

Dromiceiomimus

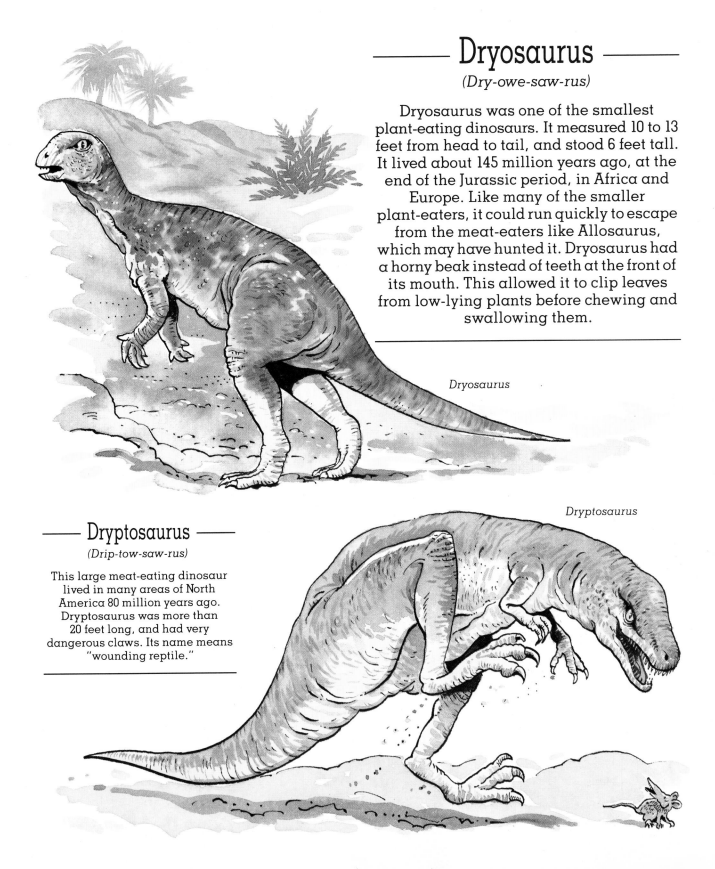

Dryosaurus
(Dry-owe-saw-rus)

Dryosaurus was one of the smallest plant-eating dinosaurs. It measured 10 to 13 feet from head to tail, and stood 6 feet tall. It lived about 145 million years ago, at the end of the Jurassic period, in Africa and Europe. Like many of the smaller plant-eaters, it could run quickly to escape from the meat-eaters like Allosaurus, which may have hunted it. Dryosaurus had a horny beak instead of teeth at the front of its mouth. This allowed it to clip leaves from low-lying plants before chewing and swallowing them.

Dryosaurus

Dryptosaurus

Dryptosaurus
(Drip-tow-saw-rus)

This large meat-eating dinosaur lived in many areas of North America 80 million years ago. Dryptosaurus was more than 20 feet long, and had very dangerous claws. Its name means "wounding reptile."

Ee

— Edmontosaurus —
(Ed-mon-tow-saw-rus)

This was a duck-billed dinosaur like Anatosaurus. Edmontosaurus was among the largest duck-bills, and grew up to 42 feet tall. It lived at the end of the Cretaceous period (136 to 65 million years ago) and was one of the last dinosaurs to survive.

Edmontosaurus

Elaphrosaurus

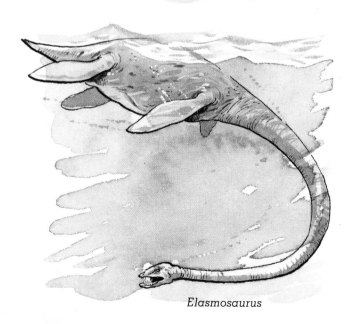

—— Elaphrosaurus ——
(Ell-aff-row-saw-rus)

Elaphrosaurus was the earliest of the "ostrich dinosaurs." It lived about 150 million years ago and may have been the ancestor of the later ostrich dinosaurs, such as Dromiceiomimus and Struthiomimus. It had shorter legs than other ostrich dinosaurs and probably could not run as fast.

—— Elasmosaurus ——
(Ell-as-mow-saw-rus)

Elasmosaurus was a large reptile that lived in the shallow seas that covered part of North America about 80 million years ago. It was not a dinosaur – these all lived on land – but belonged to a different group of reptiles. Elasmosaurus had a very long neck which could move quickly in almost any direction. At the end of the neck was a small head with a mouth full of long, sharp teeth – ideal for catching fish. Some scientists think that Elasmosaurus might also have been able to catch pterodactyls (see entry) as they flew low over the sea.

Elasmosaurus

Euskelosaurus
(You-skel-owe-saw-rus)

This large, plant-eating dinosaur lived at the end of the Triassic period (about 210 million years ago) in South Africa. The very first dinosaurs lived during this period.

Fabrosaurus
(Fab-row-saw-rus)

This small creature was one of the very first ornithischian dinosaurs. Fabrosaurus was only about 3 feet tall and walked on its hind legs. It could run away from danger quite quickly. Like all other dinosaurs in this group, Fabrosaurus ate plants. It had lots of teeth shaped to grind up tough plant food. Fabrosaurus lived in South Africa about 210 million years ago.

Euskelosaurus

Fabrosaurus

Gg-Hh

Gallimimus
(Gal-ee-my-mus)

Gallimimus lived 65 million years ago in central Asia. It was similar to Struthiomimus (see entry) but was larger. Gallimimus grew up to about 6 feet long, and was a powerful runner.

Gallimimus

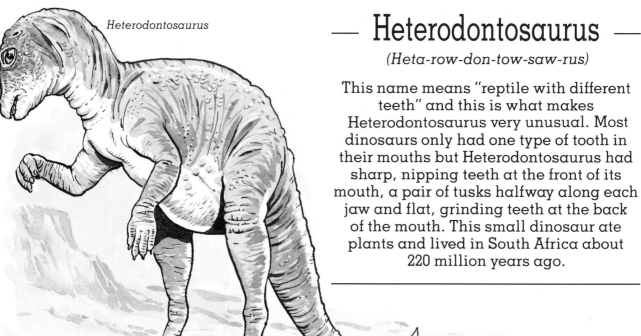

Heterodontosaurus

Heterodontosaurus
(Heta-row-don-tow-saw-rus)

This name means "reptile with different teeth" and this is what makes Heterodontosaurus very unusual. Most dinosaurs only had one type of tooth in their mouths but Heterodontosaurus had sharp, nipping teeth at the front of its mouth, a pair of tusks halfway along each jaw and flat, grinding teeth at the back of the mouth. This small dinosaur ate plants and lived in South Africa about 220 million years ago.

—— Hylaeosaurus ——
(Hi-lay-owe-saw-rus)

Covered with thick, bony armor that had sharp spikes and thick knobs, this strange dinosaur roamed Britain during the early Cretaceous period. The experts have so far only been able to guess at what a Hylaeosaurus really looked like. This is because the skeleton that was found is still set in a block of stone.

—— Hypsilophodon ——
(Hip-sill-off-owe-don)

Hypsilophodon was more than 6 feet tall, and lived 130 million years ago in Britain and Europe. Its name means "high ridged tooth." In fact, the teeth are the most-often-found fossils of this dinosaur. Hypsilophodon ate plants and could run quite quickly on its hind legs, using its tail to aid balance.

Hylaeosaurus

Hypsilophodon

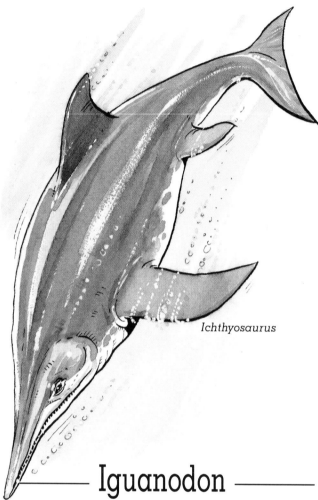

Ichthyosaurus

— Ichthyosaurus —
(Ick-thee-owe-saw-rus)

This reptile looked like a dolphin and was superbly adapted to living in the sea. It could swim very quickly indeed and used its powerful tail to push itself through the water, steering with its flippers. Scientists think that it lived on a diet of fish and squid. Ichthyosaurus was different from most reptiles as it did not lay eggs. Instead, the mother kept her eggs in her body until they were ready to hatch and then gave birth to live babies. Ichthyosaurus means "fish lizard." There were many different ichthyosaurs in their family group. They lived from 210 to 80 million years ago.

Iguanodon

Iguanodon —
(Ig-you-ah-no-don)

Iguanodon is one of the best-known dinosaurs. It was one of the first discovered by scientists. Over the years dozens of Iguanodon fossils have been found across Europe, Africa, and Asia. Iguanodon was a large, two-legged dinosaur that ate plants. It was 33 feet long and lived about 120 million years ago. When feeding, Iguanodon used its long tongue to pull plants into its mouth. It moved on its hind legs when escaping from a meat-eating dinosaur or when feeding on trees. Iguanodon had large, sharp spikes on its thumbs which scientists think may have been used as weapons.

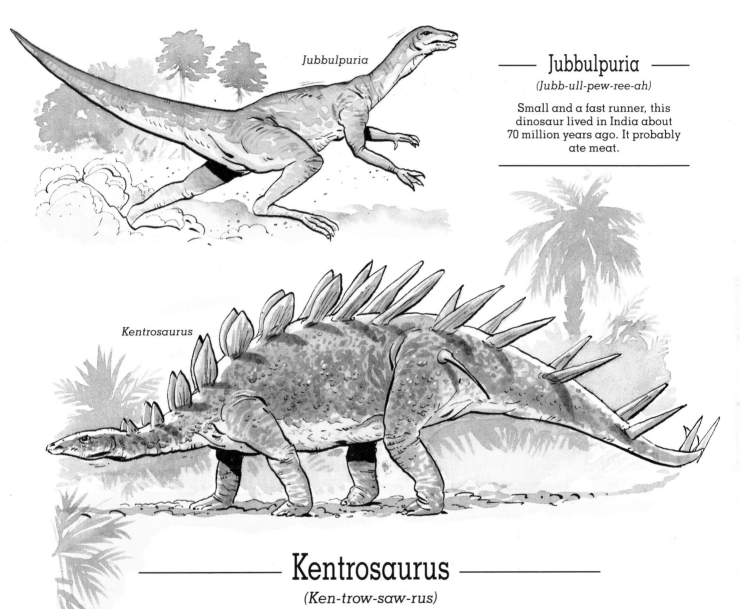

Jubbulpuria

Kentrosaurus

Jubbulpuria
(Jubb-ull-pew-ree-ah)

Small and a fast runner, this dinosaur lived in India about 70 million years ago. It probably ate meat.

Kentrosaurus
(Ken-trow-saw-rus)

This armor-plated dinosaur was 8 feet long and lived about 145 million years ago in Africa. It moved slowly – in fact, you could probably run faster than a Kentrosaurus!
It plodded around munching on low-growing plants, such as ferns. Kentrosaurus had impressive spikes and plates along its back which probably helped to protect it from large meat-eating dinosaurs. Scientists think that the plates were covered with skin. If Kentrosaurus became too hot it could stand sideways in a breeze. This would have cooled the blood in the skin over the plates. Also if Kentrosaurus became too cool it could turn its plates to face the sun and get warm.

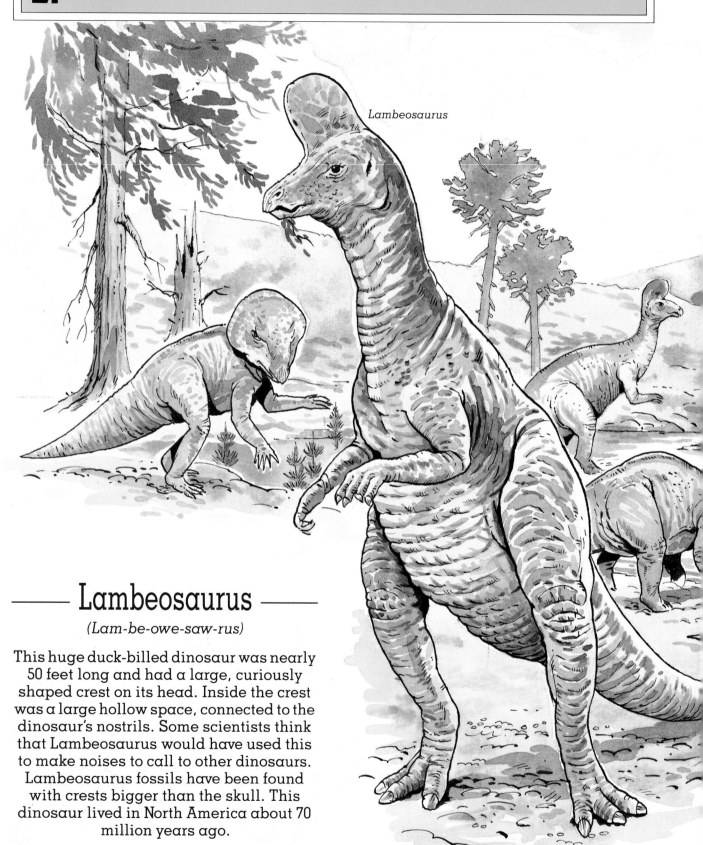

Lambeosaurus

— Lambeosaurus —

(Lam-be-owe-saw-rus)

This huge duck-billed dinosaur was nearly 50 feet long and had a large, curiously shaped crest on its head. Inside the crest was a large hollow space, connected to the dinosaur's nostrils. Some scientists think that Lambeosaurus would have used this to make noises to call to other dinosaurs. Lambeosaurus fossils have been found with crests bigger than the skull. This dinosaur lived in North America about 70 million years ago.

Leptoceratops

(Lep-tow-sir-ah-tops)

This small dinosaur was shorter than a man. It was a member of the horned dinosaur family, but it had no horns and only a very small frill around its neck! Most horned dinosaurs were large and walked on all fours, but Leptoceratops was able to run quickly on its hind legs. This strange creature lived 70 million years ago in North America.

Leptoceratops

Lufengosaurus

Lufengosaurus

(Lu-fen-go-saw-rus)

This early dinosaur was given its name because its fossils were found near Lufeng in China. It was a large plant-eater and looked very much like another dinosaur called Plateosaurus. They were probably close relatives, as they both belonged to the same family group.

Maiasaura

(May-ah-saw-rah)

When the fossils of this dinosaur were discovered in 1978, scientists became very excited. This was because they had found a fossilized nesting site. Maiasaura itself was a very ordinary duck-billed dinosaur about 29 feet long. The female Maiasaura dug a round nest and laid her eggs in it. She then stayed near the nest until the babies hatched. The young stayed in the nest while the mother Maiasaura brought food back to the nest for them to eat. Fossils show that the Maiasaura nested in large colonies of several adults and their young. This important find proved that dinosaurs looked after their babies. Maiasaura lived in North America about 70 million years ago.

Maiasaura

Mamenchisaurus

Mamenchisaurus

(Mam-en-key-saw-rus)

This extraordinary dinosaur had the longest neck of any animal. The neck measured 33 feet long and made up almost half the total length of this large plant-eater. Mamenchisaurus lived 140 million years ago in China.

Megalosaurus

(Meg-al-owe-saw-rus)

Megalosaurus fossils were the first to be recognized as bones belonging to a large, extinct reptile. The fossils were studied in Britain in 1824 by William Buckland. Megalosaurus means "big lizard." It was a large, powerful meat-eating dinosaur that lived in Europe about 140 million years ago.

Megalosaurus

— Melanorosaurus —

(Mel-an-ore-row-saw-rus)

This large plant-eating dinosaur lived about 200 million years ago in South Africa. Melanorosaurus was about twice as large and much more heavily built than its relative, Plateosaurus.

Melanorosaurus

Metriorhynchus —

(Met-ree-ore-ring-cus)

In the middle of the Jurassic period, about 160 million years ago, a group of crocodiles lived in the sea. The best-known of these was Metriorhynchus. This crocodile was 8 feet long and was well adapted to swimming. Its body was smooth and streamlined so that it could glide through the water. The long tail was powered by strong muscles and ended in a broad pair of fins. Each leg was a sturdy paddle. Metriorhynchus fed on fish, which it caught with its sharp teeth.

Metriorhynchus

Mm

Monoclonius
(Mon-owe-clow-nee-us)

Monoclonius was a horned dinosaur about 20 feet long. It had a single horn that grew from its nose, and a bony frill that extended over its neck. Monoclonius lived about 74 million years ago in North America.

Monoclonius

Morganucodon
(Mor-ga-new-co-don)

Unlike dinosaurs, which were reptiles, Morganucodon was one of the first mammals, which lived about 200 million years ago. Today, most of the largest animals, including people, are mammals. The only mammals alive at the same time as the dinosaurs were small animals such as Morganucodon. Scientists have found the fossils of several other mammals that lived alongside the dinosaurs. They were all small, furry creatures that looked like rats. These early mammals probably hunted insects or small lizards, perhaps at nighttime. The mammals took over after the dinosaurs had died out.

Morganucodon

Mosasaurus

(Mows-ah-saw-rus)

During the Cretaceous period (135 to 65 million years ago) a group of lizards, known as mosasaurs, lived in the sea and many members of this group grew to be as large as modern whales. Mosasaurus had a long, thin body which it swished from side to side to move through the water. Its long tail was flat to help it swim efficiently. The four legs were shaped like paddles and helped to steer the animal. Mosasaurus had a mouth full of sharp, round teeth. These were very strong and were ideal for biting its prey – shell-covered animals called ammonites that are now also extinct.

Mosasaurus

Muttaburrasaurus

Muttaburrasaurus

(Mut-ter-burr-ah-saw-rus)

This dinosaur's name means "reptile from Muttaburra." Its fossils were found near the town of Muttaburra in Australia. Muttaburrasaurus was 23 feet long and stood twice as tall as a man. It had sharp teeth with which to slice up its food. Scientists think that it may have eaten some meat, as well as plants. This makes it different from the dinosaurs to which it is related, such as Iguanodon and Ouranosaurus, which only ate plants. Muttaburrasaurus lived 100 million years ago.

Nodosaurus
(Nod-owe-saw-rus)

Nodosaurus was an armored dinosaur that lived in North America about 95 million years ago. The nodules of armor on its body gave it its name. Unlike most armored dinosaurs, Nodosaurus had no spikes or tail club.

Nodosaurus

— Opisthocoelicaudia —
(Oh-pis-thow-see-lic-ord-ee-ah)

Opisthocoelicaudia was an unusual sauropod dinosaur. Its tail was so strong that scientists think it was used as a support when the dinosaur reared up on its hind legs. In this way, the creature could reach high into trees. This dinosaur was 39 feet long and lived 70 million years ago in central Asia.

— Ornithomimus —
(Ore-nith-owe-my-mus)

Slightly taller than a man, this dinosaur lived 70 million years ago in North America. Like all ostrich dinosaurs, Ornithomimus had no teeth. Instead, it had a tough, horny beak that was similar to that of a modern bird. It could run away from danger very quickly.

Ornithomimus

Opisthocoelicaudia

Ouranosaurus
(Our-an-owe-saw-rus)

Ouranosaurus was very similar to Iguanodon, but had one unusual feature – a tall row of narrow spines along its back. Scientists think that these spines were covered with skin to form a sail that was used to control its temperature. If Ouranosaurus was too cold it could bask in the sun, using the sail to soak up the heat. If it was too warm, it could use the sail to catch a breeze and cool down. Ouranosaurus was 23 feet long, and lived 105 million years ago in West Africa.

Ouranosaurus

Oviraptor

Oviraptor
(Oh-veer-ap-tor)

This dinosaur was slightly smaller than a man. It had short, strong jaws, useful for crushing hard objects. Scientists think that Oviraptor may have eaten the eggs of other dinosaurs. Its name means "egg thief." Oviraptor lived 70 million years ago in Mongolia.

Pp

— Pachycephalosaurus —
(Pack-ee-sef-al-owe-saw-rus)

This dinosaur's name means "reptile with a thick head." In fact, the bone on the top of its skull was 10 inches thick. Scientists think that Pachycephalosaurus may have used its thick skull in head-butting contests. Two rival dinosaurs would have run toward each other with their heads down. When the dinosaurs hit each other, the thick skull would have acted like a crash helmet. Pachycephalosaurus was 26 feet long, ate plants, and lived in North America about 70 million years ago, during the late Cretaceous period.

Pachycephalosaurus

— Palaeoscinus —
(Pal-ee-owe-sky-nus)

This armored dinosaur was longer than a car. Its back was covered with many bony plates, and large spikes stuck out from its sides. Palaeoscinus was well protected from the attacks of meat-eating dinosaurs.

Palaeoscinus

Parasaurolophus

Parasaurolophus

(Par-ah-saw-rol-owe-fus)

Like other duck-billed dinosaurs, Parasaurolophus had a long bony crest on top of its head. However, this creature's crest was one of the largest. It stuck out for more than 3 feet behind the skull. The crest was hollow and contained air tubes running from the nostrils to the lungs. Some scientists think that the dinosaurs used them to make loud bellowing noises while others believe that the long air passages gave these dinosaurs a good sense of smell. Another idea is that the crests may have been brightly colored and used for display signals.

Phobosuchus

Phobosuchus

(Fow-bow-such-us)

The Cretaceous period (135 to 65 million years ago) saw the appearance of the first modern crocodiles. One of these, Phobosuchus, was larger than many dinosaurs. It was four times as long as the largest modern crocodile and it was a fearsome predator which would have attacked and eaten dinosaurs.

Pinacosaurus

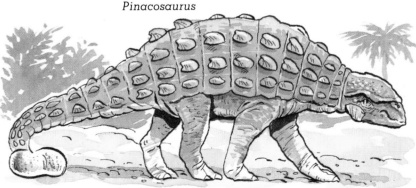

Pinacosaurus

(Pee-nah-co-saw-rus)

This armored dinosaur lived about 80 million years ago in Mongolia. Like Ankylosaurus, Pinacosaurus had a club of bone at the end of its tail with which to defend itself.

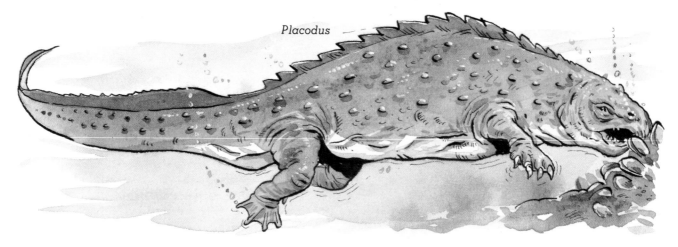

Placodus

Placodus
(Plac-oh-dus)

Placodus was not a dinosaur, but was a reptile that lived in the sea. It was able to swim well with its powerful tail and had tough, bony armor on its back. It had forward-pointing teeth at the front of its mouth which it used to pluck shellfish from rocks on the seabed, and large, flat teeth at the back of its mouth with which to crush them. Placodus lived in Europe during the late Triassic period, 225 to 195 million years ago.

Plateosaurus

Plateosaurus
(Plat-ee-owe-saw-rus)

This plant-eating dinosaur lived in Europe about 210 million years ago. It grew up to 26 feet long and could walk on all fours or on its hind legs. Plateosaurus may have used its large claws to dig up roots or to pull foliage from plants. Plateosaurus must have been a common animal because dozens of skeletons have been found by scientists.

Pliosaurus

Plesiosaurus

—— Plesiosaurus ——
(Plea-see-owe-saw-rus)

There are many different plesiosaurs but they were all very similar. From the picture you can see that Plesiosaurus had a broad body, short tail, and a long neck. Plesiosaurs used their broad flippers to push themselves through the water. They could not swim quickly, but were very agile. A plesiosaur could change direction suddenly, and the long neck could be swiftly darted in different directions. Scientists think that a plesiosaur swam on the surface of the sea hunting for fish. When it found some fish, it would dart its head toward them and snap them up in its mouth. Though they were reptiles, plesiosaurs were not dinosaurs.

—— Pliosaurus ——
(Plea-owe-saw-rus)

Pliosaurs were descended from early types of plesiosaur. The bodies of the two types of reptiles were very similar, but pliosaurs had short necks and large heads, like Pliosaurus, shown above. Pliosaurs could swim much more quickly than plesiosaurs. They used their strong flippers to power themselves through the water. We think pliosaurs ate creatures called cephalopods, which looked like squids with shells. Like plesiosaurs, pliosaurs died out towards the end of the Cretaceous period, about 65 million years ago.

Pp

Protoceratops
(Pro-tow-sir-ah-tops)

This small dinosaur was not much larger than a big dog. It lived 80 million years ago in Mongolia and was one of the first horned dinosaurs. As you can see from the picture, it did not actually have any horns, but its large neck frill and other features put it in the same family as Triceratops and Monoclonius. Scientists have found many Protoceratops fossils in Mongolia, some of which were the remains of babies and young animals. These fossils have enabled scientists to study the way in which dinosaurs grew from eggs to adults.

Protoceratops

Psittacosaurus

Psittacosaurus
(Sit-ah-co-saw-rus)

Psittacosaurus lived about 95 million years ago in Central Asia. It might have been the ancestor of all the later horned dinosaurs. It was a small creature – only about 6 feet long. Psittacosaurus walked mainly on its hind legs, although it could also use its front legs. It had a sharp, parrot-like beak with which it could nip leaves from bushes. The back of its skull had a small frill which became bigger in later horned dinosaurs.

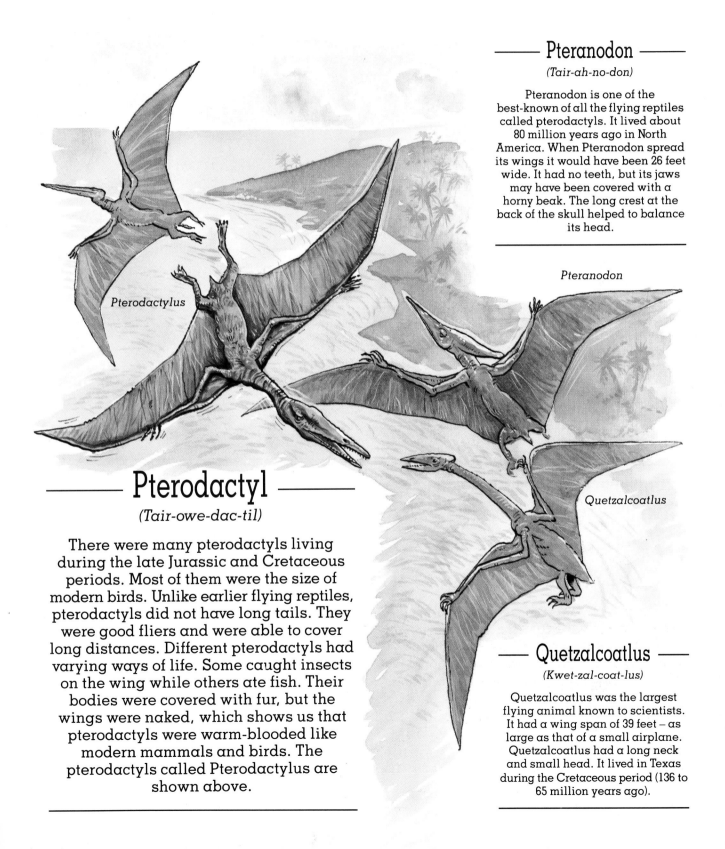

Pteranodon
(Tair-ah-no-don)

Pteranodon is one of the best-known of all the flying reptiles called pterodactyls. It lived about 80 million years ago in North America. When Pteranodon spread its wings it would have been 26 feet wide. It had no teeth, but its jaws may have been covered with a horny beak. The long crest at the back of the skull helped to balance its head.

Pteranodon

Pterodactylus

Quetzalcoatlus

Pterodactyl
(Tair-owe-dac-til)

There were many pterodactyls living during the late Jurassic and Cretaceous periods. Most of them were the size of modern birds. Unlike earlier flying reptiles, pterodactyls did not have long tails. They were good fliers and were able to cover long distances. Different pterodactyls had varying ways of life. Some caught insects on the wing while others ate fish. Their bodies were covered with fur, but the wings were naked, which shows us that pterodactyls were warm-blooded like modern mammals and birds. The pterodactyls called Pterodactylus are shown above.

Quetzalcoatlus
(Kwet-zal-coat-lus)

Quetzalcoatlus was the largest flying animal known to scientists. It had a wing span of 39 feet – as large as that of a small airplane. Quetzalcoatlus had a long neck and small head. It lived in Texas during the Cretaceous period (136 to 65 million years ago).

Rhamphorhynchus

— Rhamphorhynchus —
(Ram-for-ring-cus)

During the Jurassic period the air was ruled by various types of Rhamphorhynchus. Its name means "narrow beak." Like pterodactyls, these flying reptiles had bodies which were covered with fur. They had long, bony tails which ended in a flap of skin. This may have been used as a rudder to steer it when flying.

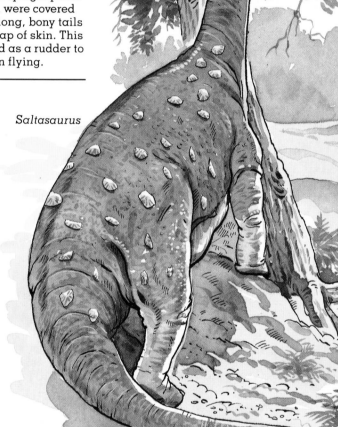

Saltasaurus

—— Saltasaurus ——
(Salt-ah-saw-rus)

Saltasaurus was 39 feet long and nearly twice as tall as a man when measured to its shoulder. It lived about 65 million years ago and was one of the very last dinosaurs. The fossils of this dinosaur were found in the Salta province, an area of Argentina. This was a rare find as it was covered with thousands of pieces of bony armor.

Saltopus

— Saltopus —
(Salt-owe-pus)

This was an early dinosaur that lived 200 million years ago in Scotland. Saltopus was about the same size as a modern cat and may have lived in a similar way. Scientists think that Saltopus ate small lizards and mammals.

Saurolophus

Saurolophus
(Saw-rol-owe-fus)

Saurolophus lived 65 million years ago and was a plant-eating, duck-billed dinosaur which would have stood about 30 feet tall. Fossil remains have been found in both North America and Eastern Asia. It had a much smaller crest than some of the other duck-billed dinosaurs such as Parasaurolophus and Corythosaurus. Saurolophus had a typical duck-billed dinosaur's body, with webbed fingers and a powerful tail. These would have made Saurolophus a good swimmer. It may have escaped from meat-eating dinosaurs by swimming into deep water.

Saurornithoides

Saurornithoides
(Saw-ror-nith-oy-dees)

With its long legs, Saurornithoides was obviously a fast runner. It had a fourth claw on each hind foot, which was probably held clear of the ground and may have been used to attack other animals. Its hands had three claws that could have been used to hold small pieces of food. This dinosaur had very large eyes which would have been useful when hunting at dusk. For a dinosaur of its size – it was about 6 feet tall – it had a surprisingly large brain. Saurornithoides lived about 80 million years ago and was found in Mongolia.

—— Scelidosaurus ——
(Skel-id-owe-saw-rus)

This early ornithischian (bird-hipped) plant-eater lived in England about 180 million years ago. In some ways it resembled armored dinosaurs such as Ankylosaurus, but it was also similar to plated dinosaurs such as Stegosaurus. Some scientists think that Scelidosaurus was the ancestor of both groups of dinosaurs while others put Scelidosaurus in a group of its own. It grew to 13 feet long, was rather heavy, and walked slowly on all four legs. Rows of bony knobs ran along its body and offered protection against attack from meat-eating dinosaurs.

Scelidosaurus

Scutellosaurus

—— Scutellosaurus ——
(Skut-ell-owe-saw-rus)

Scutellosaurus lived in North America nearly 200 million years ago. It walked on all fours most of the time, but could also run on its hind legs. Scutellosaurus had a very long tail and its back was covered with many protective bony plates.

—— Segisaurus ——
(Seg-ee-saw-rus)

Only slightly bigger than a turkey, this small, fast-running dinosaur lived 185 million years ago in North America. It probably ate lizards and large insects. The fossils of Segisaurus puzzle scientists because some of the bones are very unusual.

Segisaurus

—— Silvisaurus ——
(Sill-vee-saw-rus)

Another of the armored dinosaurs, Silvisaurus was 13 feet long and it lived 95 million years ago in North America. Its back was covered with flat plates of bone that joined together into a solid shield. Sharp spines stuck out sideways from the shoulders and the end of its tail.

Silvisaurus

Spinosaurus

Spinosaurus
(Spy-no-saw-rus)

Fossil remains of this dinosaur were found in Egypt. It was a large meat-eater and was 40 feet long. It had a long row of spines along its back joined together by a flap of skin. The largest of these spines was taller than a man. The skin made a large sail that could have broken easily. This means Spinosaurus was unlikely to have hunted large animals. It probably scavenged meat from dinosaurs that had already died or that had been killed by other meat-eaters. Spinosaurus probably used its sail in the same way as Ouranosaurus. It lived 110 million years ago.

Staurikosaurus

Staurikosaurus

(Stor-rick-owe-saw-rus)

This was one of the earliest dinosaurs ever to have roamed the Earth. It was small – only 6 feet from tip to toe – but could run quickly on its hind legs. The front legs were rather short, which shows that Staurikosaurus probably used them for grasping food rather than walking. It had sharp teeth, which means that it probably ate meat. Scientists are not sure whether Staurikosaurus was related to small meat-eaters such as Saltopus or to plant-eaters like Plateosaurus. It lived in South America during the Triassic period.

Stegoceras

(Steg-oss-err-as)

Stegoceras was a bone-head dinosaur, like Pachycephalosaurus. It was one of the smaller members of this group, being only 6 feet long. It would have fought other Stegoceras by head-butting, using its thick skull to take the force of the impact. Stegoceras lived 75 million years ago in China.

Stegoceras

Stegosaurus

Stegosaurus
(Steg-owe-saw-rus)

Probably the largest plated dinosaur, Stegosaurus was twice as tall as a man and grew up to 24 feet long. Two rows of bony plates ran along the back of this dinosaur. They were probably used to control its body heat. The sharp spines on Stegosaurus's tail would have been used against any attacking meat-eating dinosaur. This plant-eating dinosaur lived in North America 140 million years ago.

Stenonychosaurus
(Sten-on-ick-owe-saw-rus)

Stenonychosaurus was closely related to Saurornithoides, but it was even "brainier." In proportion to its body weight, Stenonychosaurus had a larger brain than any other dinosaur. Stenonychosaurus lived about 80 million years ago in North America.

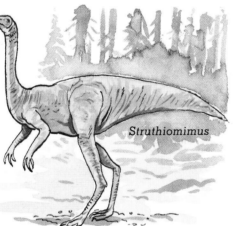

Struthiomimus

Struthiomimus
(Strew-thee-owe-my-mus)

The name Struthiomimus means "ostrich mimic." It looked like an ostrich without feathers. It had a compact body, long neck, a toothless mouth, and long legs. It was able to run very quickly. It lived 75 million years ago in North America.

Stenonychosaurus

Styracosaurus
(Sty-rack-owe-saw-rus)

Styracosaurus was a medium-sized, horned dinosaur that lived about 80 million years ago. Styracosaurus had a single horn on its nose and a number of other spines growing from its neck frill.

Styracosaurus

Tarbosaurus

Tarbosaurus
(Tar-bow-saw-rus)

Tarbosaurus was a huge, meat-eating dinosaur. It was 45 feet long and must have been a very powerful dinosaur. One strange feature was the size of its arms, which were tiny compared to the rest of the animal. Some scientists think that they helped Tarbosaurus to stand up. When lying down on its stomach, Tarbosaurus would dig its arms into the ground to use as levers. By pushing with its hind legs, Tarbosaurus would then be able to stand up.

Tenontosaurus
(Ten-on-tow-saw-rus)

The most remarkable feature of this plant-eating dinosaur was its long tail. The tail might have been a useful defense against its enemies. Tenontosaurus lived 110 million years ago in North America.

Tenontosaurus

Thecodontosaurus

Thecodontosaurus
(Thee-co-don-tow-saw-rus)

Thecodontosaurus was an early plant-eating dinosaur. It was about the size of a large dog. Thecodontosaurus lived in Britain about 205 million years ago.

Thescelosaurus

— Thescelosaurus —

(Thess-kel-owe-saw-rus)

Thescelosaurus lived in North America about 65 million years ago, just before all the dinosaurs died out. It was a plant-eater and stood as tall as a man. Thescelosaurus may have escaped from attackers by running quickly away on its hind legs, but it also had bony studs set into its skin as protection.

Torosaurus

— Torosaurus —

(Tor-row-saw-rus)

This huge, horned dinosaur lived 65 million years ago right at the end of the Mesozoic era. Like all horned dinosaurs, Torosaurus was a plant-eater. Its horns were used both to defend itself from meat-eating dinosaurs and to fight rival Torosaurus. The bony neck frill was a base for its powerful jaw muscles. At over 5 feet long, Torosaurus's skull is larger than that of any other known land animal.

Tt

Tyrannosaurus

Triceratops

Triceratops

(Tri-sir-ah-tops)

Triceratops was a large, horned dinosaur that lived in North America. At 30 feet long and weighing up to 5.4 tons, it was about the size of a small truck. It lived about 65 million years ago during the Cretaceous period. Triceratops ate plants, biting the leaves with its sharp teeth. It had three large horns on its head which were useful protection from the large meat-eating dinosaurs of the time.

Tyrannosaurus

(Tie-ran-owe-saw-rus)

Tyrannosaurus was the biggest meat-eating dinosaur of all time. It was about 46 feet long and stood over 16 feet high. You can see that Tyrannosaurus had powerful claws on its hind legs. It may have used these to fight other dinosaurs and to kill them for food. Tyrannosaurus's teeth were the size of a human hand. Some scientists think that Tyrannosaurus fed on the bodies of dead dinosaurs, as it was too slow to catch its own food.

"Ultrasaurus"
(Ul-tra-saw-rus)

As this unofficial name suggests, "Ultrasaurus" was truly enormous. Its fossils have only recently been found and scientists have not yet had time to study them properly. It seems that "Ultrasaurus" was similar to Brachiosaurus, but it was even larger. It would have been 98 feet long, and tall enough to look over the top of a four-story building. "Ultrasaurus" may have been the largest animal ever to have lived on earth.

Ultrasaurus

Velociraptor

Velociraptor
(Vel-owe-sir-ap-tor)

This dinosaur was smaller than a man and lived in Mongolia 75 million years ago. It was a meat-eating dinosaur that attacked other animals with the sharp, hooked claws on its hind legs.

Ww-Yy-Zz

Wannanosaurus

— Wannanosaurus —
(Wan-an-owe-saw-rus)

Wannanosaurus lived in China during the Cretaceous period. Its name means "reptile from Wannan." It was a bone-head dinosaur, like Stegoceras.

Yangchuanosaurus

— Yangchuanosaurus —
(Yan-chew-an-owe-saw-rus)

This powerful hunter lived 145 million years ago in China. It was nearly three times as long as a car and had strong legs. Yangchuanosaurus was a relative of Allosaurus and could probably run quickly. It would have been able to attack and eat large dinosaurs. Its fossil skeleton was discovered in 1978.

Zephyrosaurus

— Zephyrosaurus —
(Zeff-ear-owe-saw-rus)

This two-legged dinosaur lived 120 million years ago in North America. Zephyrosaurus meant "the reptile of the wind." It was 6 feet long and ate plants.